I Can Do It!

Copyright © 1985 by Karen Erickson and Maureen Roffey. All rights reserved. Produced for the publishers by Sadie Fields Productions Ltd, London. First published in the United States by Scholastic Inc.

12 11 10 9 8 7 6 5 4 3 2 1   2   5 6 7 8 9 / 8

Printed and bound by
L.E.G.O., Vicenza, Italy

I Can Get Organized

Karen Erickson and Maureen Roffey

Scholastic Inc.

New York Toronto London Auckland Sydney Tokyo

Everything is so mixed up.

Who put my shoes in the
refrigerator?

How did my toothbrush end
up under the dining room table?

Why is my truck in the
kitchen sink?

I'll never get things back in their places. Everything is too messy.

My poor room. It would take
forever to clean this room.
I can't do it. I'm too little.

But who's going to do it?

Maybe I'll just start.
Maybe I can do it! Pick up.
Put away. Get organized.

Pick up. Put away.

Pick up. Put away.

Look. I'm organized.

I can do it!
I did it!

I · CAN · DO · IT · BOOKS
I Can Get Organized

I Can Settle Down

I Can Share

I Can Do Something
When There's Nothing To Do